PRAYERS AND WISDOM

of a

FATHER

Steven W. Lyle

AuthorHouse™
1663 Liberty Drive
Bloomington, IN 47403
www.authorhouse.com
Phone: 1 (800) 839-8640

Published by AuthorHouse 09/12/2016

ISBN: 978-1-5246-0823-1 (sc)
ISBN: 978-1-5246-0825-5 (hc)
ISBN: 978-1-5246-0824-8 (e)

Library of Congress Control Number: 2016907649

Print information available on the last page.

authorHOUSE®

Preface

Having lost my father at an early age, I did not have someone who could show me what that role called father or dad was all about.

It wasn't until I became a father that I realized that whatever that role was, I wanted and needed to get it right.

It was then through the influence of a church that I started to look upward for my fatherly direction, guidance, council, comfort, and strength. Through three decades of prayer, my heavenly Father—the Father I prayed to—became my earthly father as well. Through his son, Jesus, I began to offer my prayers of thanksgiving, my prayer requests, my prayers of hope, and my prayers for strength to him.

What started out as prayers became conversations where I would pray and just listen for his still, small voice and the sense of his presence around me. A calm and peaceful feeling always comes to me after I pray—a sensation that I cannot explain.

What I *can* explain is that I want that calm and peaceful feeling for my sons and their children because for me it has made all the difference in my life-journey.

Epigraph

Each day is God's gift to you.
What you do with it is your gift to Him.

—T. D. Jakes

Contents

I would like to thank my heavenly Father for his constant watch over me and for his abundant grace that he has shown me. I continue to ask him, as the only father I have known, to watch over my children and their children as he has watched over me.

I would also like to thank my two sons, Paul Steven Lyle and Brandon Wayne Lyle, who serve as the inspiration for this book. One of the biggest joys of my life has been to see the two of them become the fine men that they are today. They both have a strong sense of self and a strong faith. What more could a father ask for?

To them, I dedicate this book.

Steven is pictured above with (from left to right) his grandson, Logan Christian Lyle, his son Paul Steven Lyle (Logan's father), and his son Brandon Wayne Lyle.

Introduction

God holds you accountable for your own spiritual life. Living a life of faith and integrity and then passing it on is the responsibility of the faithful and of a parent.

This book represents excerpts from a collection of prayers and thoughts that I wrote and compiled over several years for my two sons. Each Christmas I would organize the prayers and thoughts into themes. I would print them out and put them in a clear document holder, roll them up, and tie red and green ribbons around them. I would then place them in their stockings.

It was my hope that the prayers and thoughts that I had written and prayed throughout the years would give them strength and hope. But most of all, I hoped that the prayers would increase their own desire to take time to pray each day.

During the most difficult moments of our lives, and in those times when we are down on ourselves and feeling broken for whatever reason, I believe that it is life-changing to know that the amazing, self-sacrificing, wonderful love of God will never turn away from the one who reaches out to him.

The only Father I have ever truly known is my heavenly Father, and he has never abandoned me. He has not always been happy with me, but he has always been there. It has been my hope that I could possibly be a mere fraction of that kind of father to my sons as he has been and is to me.

As the years have gone by, I have had those moments in my life in which I could sense God (my Father) smiling down on me and every fiber of my being was strengthened. I experienced this often as I had tried doing something that I had no idea how to do, but somehow my heavenly Father saw me through. During those moments I felt his approval as my young sons felt with me. It was as if I could hear him say, "Good job, son; I am proud of you."

At other times, after something not so good happened that I caused, he would have to break through to me and show me how badly I'd messed up. He would allow me to experience my feelings of failure, remorse, and regret. But then after a period of feeling broken, there came a sense of restoration and real renewal. It was as if God held me to his chest and wiped my tears away, then gently kissed my forehead to reassure me that his love was ever strong.

I want the gentle smile of God upon whatever my sons are doing and trying to do in their lives. I know it will give them the extra strength that will help them succeed.

A good father acknowledges mistakes as well as successes and loves you through it all. Some of that love is tough love with periods of silence for reflection, but nonetheless it's a constant and real everlasting love.

There have been many times in my life that I have felt like I had come to the end of my strength and abilities and felt my faith tested. In those times, I needed strength that rest and nutrition cannot give. I needed the strength that comes from God alone. I needed to sit for a moment and be silent and listen for God's still, small voice of reassurance telling me, "I am with you; you have nothing to fear." I would then be renewed, revived, and ready to try again. That is what prayer does for me, and that is what I hope it will offer to my sons throughout their lives.

Each day, and until my Father calls me home, I open up my morning prayer to God thanking him for giving me two sons—two sons that I am so proud of and thankful for. I ask him to guide their efforts and to bless them. I ask him to keep them healthy, safe, and free from harm. I ask him to keep them focused on the things that strengthen their lives and their characters. I ask him to watch over them as he has watched over me. I ask him for his guidance to help me help them as they move forward in their lives.

People should never succumb to others making them live their lives beneath the aspirations that God has for them. We should always attempt to dream our dreams into our lives and drive passionately into those lives, always making prayer a part of them.

Prayer has the power to change our lives for the better, and it can transform us. It is my prayer that my sons will commit time to pray each day, if only for a moment—even if it is a short prayer. One short prayer that has only two words yet carries so much meaning is to just close your eyes and say, "Thank you."

Believe in the Power of Prayer

Prayer is

meant to be experienced, embraced, reflected upon, and accepted for the marvelous mystery that it is.

Prayer is about surrender.

Through prayer, you learn to discern
what you need to do for yourself and what you must
entrust to God's realm and life's serendipity.

Prayer is

a spiritual language through which the Spirit flows. Jesus taught us that. He talked with God, named his needs and fears, and ultimately received the strength to fulfill his mission.

I pray that through

having a relationship with God

you

can find the real significance

in your life.

If you sincerely want to choose

a better path

than the one you are on,

start that path

on your knees in prayer.

God will help you make conscious decisions to be on that

better path.

Trust him.

I pray that you will lift up your greatest concerns

to God

and allow him to bring peace

in your heart and life to your life.

Remember

that no matter how big or small you think the problem or situation is,

like a good father,

everything is important to God.

Be grateful

I pray that you will make a list

of all the things for which you are grateful

and that you reflect on it

often,

especially when you are feeling down.

It can be

life-changing.

I pray that each and every day

you cultivate a grateful, kind, and cheerful heart

and that you celebrate life

for what it is:

an amazing gift from God.

Each day,

in the midst of your busy and hectic schedule,

I pray that you can stop long enough

to be grateful.

We all find ourselves in difficult times.

That is just life.

I pray that even in the midst of your difficulties

you will be able to say

"Thank you"

to God for all the wondrous things he has done

and will do in your life.

Think positive

———————— ✦ ✦ ◆ ✦ ✦ ————————

I pray that you will

focus on, attend to, and expend energy

on what you want to define you.

I pray that your definition

is positive and uplifting

to you

and to others.

Thinking negative thoughts

(about yourself or others)

and

expending energy on them

is a waste of time.

Negative thoughts will come,

and it is okay to acknowledge them briefly—

but get rid of them quickly.

They are

life-draining.

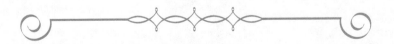

I pray that your positive thoughts become actions

for your actions have

the ability and opportunity to touch

the lives of others

in meaningful ways.

Be kind

I pray that you

will treat everyone and everything

with dignity and respect

and that you

develop genuine relationships

in your life.

Please remember that the kind thing you do

for someone may be

the only kindness that person experiences that day,

or perhaps in his or her life.

Don't underestimate the impact your actions have.

Make them count.

Sometimes

just a smile will make someone else's day.

Don't be afraid

to be generous with

your smiles.

Surround yourself
with
kind and positive people

◆ ◆ ◆ ◆ ◆

It is important

while being positive ourselves

to surround ourselves with positive people.

I pray that you will do this.

Positive people

are those individuals whose very presence

helps us stay centered on what is right and good.

The kindness of such people

can only guide you toward being kind to others

as well as teaching you to

love yourself.

Move away from people

in your life

who want to fuel negative thoughts

as they will

build up negative energy.

Pray that God

will help them.

It is usually the case that you cannot change

their negative orientation.

However, you can give them an example
of a positive outlook.

Be authentic

I pray that you will be authentic in all that you do.

Share feelings, be honest, and talk

about what really matters.

Don't have pretense and try to impress.

If someone does not like your authentic self, move on from

that interaction or relationship.

I pray that throughout your life

you

make decisions

based on

authenticity.

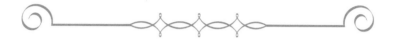

Remember that an authentic self

is most impressive,

and God loves you

just as you are.

Look for guidance

I pray that you don't try to figure out everything on your own.

Listen for God's voice

in everything you do and everywhere you go.

He will keep you on track

if you look to him for guidance.

No matter how small you think the request is,

God takes it very seriously.

When you are at a crossroads

and just not sure if you should go left or right,

I pray that you look up and sit in silence.

You will get your answer.

It will not be like a burning bush

but more of a peace that you will experience that will lead to

clarity in your mind

on the direction you need to take.

Needing guidance or help with something

after you have done your

absolute best

is not a sign of weakness.

Not asking for the guidance or help

is weakness.

Take responsibility

—————— ◆ ◆ ◆ ◆ ◆ ——————

I pray that you will realize

that the only person you can change is yourself,

not others.

I pray that you always take responsibility

for your attitude, your perceptions,

and

your corresponding actions.

Remember that no one can make you happy

except you,

and you are not responsible

for someone else's happiness; he or she is.

What we can do is create happiness for ourselves

and share it with others.

When you are given responsibility for something

big or small,

take it seriously and see it through.

Trust

I pray that you will trust God

in all of your circumstances—the good times, the
bad times, and the times in between.

Peace is not always the absence of struggles or challenges

but rather knowing that God loves you

and gives you strength to find peace and comfort

in the midst of life's trials.

Trust him.

I pray that you will be intentional about practicing trust.

Make a decision to trust someone, something, or yourself

after you have asked God for guidance.

If you find that the trust has been broken,

at least you made an effort

and will know more about where

to not put your trust.

As you interact with others,

the only way for them to trust you

is for you to be trustworthy.

Having someone trust you is a gift from God.

Treat it that way.

Be forgiving

I pray that you will practice forgiveness

when someone has wronged you

and that you

will ask for forgiveness when you have wronged someone.

Forgiveness brings healing

to all parties.

It restores relationships and cultivates grateful spirits.

God forgives our sins,

and we most forgive others and ourselves.

Forgiveness

gives us the capacity to make a new start.

I pray that you will not deny yourself

or others

that fresh start.

Don't expect forgiveness to be easy.

It is not.

However, it is well worth the effort.

Be courageous

I pray that you will always be strong and courageous

when faced with difficult situations and choices

and that you

know that God will help you do what is best.

Courage and bravery are not just demonstrated

on the battlefield

but can be found wherever people push

to make positive change.

I pray that when you find yourself in an uncomfortable

situation

and you need help to figure out how to address it,

you will allow God

to work through you and strengthen you with the courage

to take the necessary

right steps forward.

God tells us to be strong and of good courage.

If you are doing good work

and

doing the right things

while staying focused on positive outcomes,

God will strengthen your heart and your resolve.

Face your fears

I pray that you will not rob yourself of life and joy

by living in fear and worry.

Let God help you ease your mind.

Fear and uncertainty will come. Just look up and
know that God is ready to ease the burden.

Lift up your fears to him in prayer, and you will be amazed

by what you will experience.

Fear can actually be a friend to you

as it helps to keep you from potentially dangerous situations.

So fear is not all bad.

God can help you discern

what is healthy fear and what is not.

I pray that God

will give you

the courage

to face your fear and doubt and

the wisdom

to listen, learn, and grow.

Don't let stress rule you

I pray that at the times in your life that you are stressed,

you will remind yourself

to rejoice in your trials so that those stressful days actually

become

character-building times.

I pray that you don't gaze off into the distance too often
stressing over situations

so you don't see the beautiful things

that are right in front of you,

such as your family, your friends, your home, and yes°… even you.

Count every new day as a gift

from God.

Don't let stress rob you

of experiencing the beauty of

this gift.

Deal with insecurities

◆•◆•◆•◆•◆

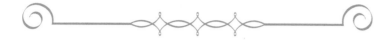

I pray

that you will remind yourself

when you feel uncertain, unsafe, or shaky

that you have two choices.

You can either focus on the circumstance

and let your mind run wild

with all the should haves and could haves,

or you can fix your eyes on God

and know that he will provide the comfort that you need.

Doubt is a nagging emotion.

Uncertainty, hesitation, indecision, and questioning

rob us of confidence.

I pray that you will not quit

because you become convinced that an upcoming task

is impossible,

or assume that you have only a given amount of intelligence,

talents, and good qualities,

or let every situation become a matter of evaluation of

yourself.

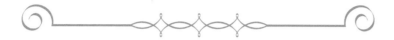

Don't be too hard on yourself,

and

believe in your capabilities.

Know that if you are continuing to seek him

and

reach out to him,

he is well pleased with you and will keep you strong

and

on the right path.

Deal with failures

Failure to do something

to the extent that it needed to be done will happen.

That is life.

The absolute, most serious mistake of failure

is to not learn from it

and

to stop trying to do better.

I pray that God does not let you miss an opportunity

to encourage someone each day.

Everyone feels failure at some point in their lives,

and the absolute best way to receive encouragement

is to give it.

When you feel you have failed yourself

or someone else,

take responsibility for it and then

go to God in prayer.

Allow him to guide you through these very real feelings.

You will be comforted, and you will receive a calmness

that will let you know

your next steps.

Persevere

❖ ◆ ◆ ◆ ❖

I pray that when it seems

that someone has shattered your hopes

and dreams,

you will pick up even the smallest of pieces

and

rebuild to create what you thought not possible.

I pray that in the midst of any sorrows,

you look up, close your eyes, and feel God's presence giving you strength

for it is in those times when his arms truly do

envelop you in comfort.

Whatever it is that you are doing

in your life,

at work, or at home,

pursue it with all the passion you have,

and you will see

the fruits of that labor if you finish what you start.

Always look forward

I pray that you never want to go

back home

to a place that no longer exists.

It's okay to have the memories, but don't let them

overshadow today.

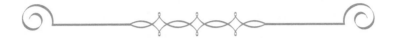

I pray that you will fix your eyes on the home

that you want to create and make it so.

Always move forward,

taking with you the lessons of the past

and

continually building for a better tomorrow.

If you do find yourself looking back, I pray that it is to reflect

on the positive aspects of your life

along with lessons you learned

from setbacks or instances where you were not your

best self.

This is the best kind of reflection.

Enjoy life

————————— ❖ ❖ ❖ ❖ —————————

I pray that you will simply enjoy the life God gives you by seeing all of the good and positive things around you. Whenever possible, enable others to do the same. There are so many good things to be thankful for.

Don't be so busy in making plans for the future

that you let your life pass you by in the present.

Remember that life is short, and the present moment

will never happen again.

We are not guaranteed tomorrow,

but we do have the present day

to make the best day of our lives

and the lives of those

we love.

Epilogue

As you grow older, I pray that the difficult times in your life will be made better through prayer and knowing that you had a father on earth who loved you dearly and a Father in heaven who loves you too.

I pray that you pass on to your sons and daughters that kind of love, that you demonstrate your love through your actions, and that you never let a chance go by to tell your children that you love them.

And remember—no matter how old they are, you can still hug them tight and thank God for their lives.

About the Author

Steven W. Lyle is the author of *The Power of Being Yourself: Navigating the Corporate World When You Are a Minority.* He is the former director of engineering workforce development and chief diversity officer of Texas Instruments. Having spent thirty-six years at Texas Instruments and raising two sons in his early years at the company, he found that prayer made all the difference when facing and embracing each day—both at home and at work.

Over the course of many years, he has said and wrote prayers for his sons that he wants to share with other parents. This book is a collection of excerpts from his prayer compilation. It is his hope that it will be inspiring for those who read them and that it will encourage readers to consider a lifelong ritual of prayer if they have not already adopted one.

Steven is a US Army veteran and received the Bronze Star during the first Gulf War. He holds double degrees from Western Kentucky University in information technology and office administration and is a graduate of the Human Resource Strategic Leadership course at the University of Michigan and the Strategic Negotiations course at Harvard.

He held various roles at Texas Instruments over his thirty-six years, including the chief information technology officer role for TI's Consumer Products Business; the director of quality for TI's Information Technology (IT) Group; the director of the first IT management consulting practice for TI's Software Business; the director of business excellence for TI's semiconductor business; and the director of worldwide staffing.

Steven has also served on various boards throughout the years, such as the UT Dallas Industry Advisory Council to the School of Engineering, the UT Dallas School of Management Industry Advisory Board, the UT Dallas Development Board, the Dallas County Community College District Foundation Board, the Career Center Advisory Board at Southern Methodist University, and the Information Systems Advisory Board at Texas Tech University. He also served on an advisory council to Catalyst, the leading nonprofit organization advocating for women in business.

Printed in the United States
By Bookmasters